Squirting: It's Easier Than You Think

A Holistic Guide to Female Pleasure
with easy tips to achieve female ejaculation

R. Leigh

Acknowledgments

Thank you to JW for the cover design and for being my partner in crime. I'm not sure what I would do without your encouragement and support. Thank you to my ex-husband (who will probably never read this book) for helping me to mistakenly discover my ability. But more so, thank you to the few men I've experienced female ejaculation with. Those men were the few gems I discovered who were patient and giving enough to take the time to focus on my pleasure, not just their own.

Foreword

My Experience
I am not an expert, yet personal experience and questions from others who know I can accomplish female ejaculation encouraged me to share my knowledge. Although admittedly I have researched the topic thoroughly.

What You Already Know
If you are reading this book, you already have a base knowledge of female ejaculation. We'll cover some basics, but this is primarily a quick guide of tips to help anyone experience female ejaculation.

My Gift
This is my gift to women. EVERY woman, everywhere should experience squirting. It's not just for porn stars, and through this short book, I hope to help you become in touch with your body and help you feel worthy of sexual pleasure.

Peaceful Water

Water has played a pivotal role in my life, as well as it seems to in others. Where many feel at peace is near or in the water. Water had provided me pleasure before...the serenity of a rainy day, the peacefulness felt when diving deep beneath the ocean waters, the cleansing feeling of water running down my naked body. It's no wonder a release of "water" from my body could provide immense sexual pleasure.

Accidental Squirter

I, like probably many others, discovered squirting by accident. I was 10 years into my marriage (unknowingly nearing divorce) with almost 20 years of sexual experience, most of it with my husband. I was in a dysfunctional relationship where healthy communication was lacking, and personal past sexual trauma affected me in such a way so I felt guilt and as though I was bad or undeserving when it came to experiencing sexual pleasure. My husband had never pleasured me in any way which achieved an orgasm. Most times I "finished" by myself via masturbation while he sat in the living room on the couch watching TV, eating a snack. The one time I squirted it was a fluke. I didn't understand what it was nor did I know a woman could ejaculate. Unusually on this particular night my husband spent a great deal of time stimulating me, resulting in a love making session which lasted several hours. I felt a great amount of pressure, unlike anything I'd ever felt before, except it felt similar to the urge to pee. A pressure that felt good, yet needed releasing. Something inside of me told me to let it go. Not only did it feel like a huge release, but it was the most satisfying orgasm I had ever had in my life.

Squirting: It's Easier Than You Think

I've been told since the experience, men feel a similar pressure before ejaculation. They can't hold it any longer. That's exactly how I felt. I felt like I was holding in urine, but if I let it go, it would be the greatest release of all time, and it was. After experiencing squirting I can understand why men enjoy sex so much, if what I felt was in any way similar to what they feel. After the first time I told my husband, "if this is what it feels like when a man ejaculates, then no wonder men enjoy sex so much." It was the ultimate release. It reinforced in my mind women are meant to enjoy sexual pleasure as much as men.

After it happened the floor was soaked, not just a little bit, but it really looked like buckets of fluid were spilled on our carpet. The sensation felt great and my husband was over the top in excitement saying "oh baby, keep cumming" and licking it off of me as it came out.

Yet the first time I squirted while it felt so good, and turned my husband on so much, we really didn't know what had happened. We weren't regular porn watchers and squirting was not in our vocabulary. After it happened I felt somewhat embarrassed, thinking maybe I HAD simply peed.

Squirting: It's Easier Than You Think

I was confused and embarrassed. What exactly had just happened? I spent the entire next day online, researching, trying to understand exactly what my body had experienced. Some sites proclaimed female ejaculation didn't even exist. But others gave a clearer picture of exactly what happened with videos and explanations. And they vehemently denied it was pee.

My husband was excited when I explained it to him and he couldn't wait for it to happen again, but it never did. My ability to feel comfortable with him was hindered. He wasn't a patient, kind lover. Having an orgasm with him during sex was hard anyways, so pushing myself to the level of squirting would likely never happen again, or rarely, if it did. At least not with him.

I could make it happen on my own since I now understood how it worked. But one of the issues we experienced as a couple which prevented me from orgasming with him in the first place was his lack of patience. It took me awhile to relax and feel comfortable. Orgasm didn't come quickly and he became impatient and frustrated which made the problem worse. It was a lot of pressure for me. In hindsight, I've learned men often feel inadequate or inept during sex, or fear they are not good enough. Most men truly want to please their partners. Other

Squirting: It's Easier Than You Think

women experience similar issues as I did, not always related to their partner, but their own inability to let go either because they have issues with their sexuality or they are worried about how they look, smell, taste, whatever. They may have a million things running through their head and they just can't stay in the moment, which is key to any orgasm.

Squirting became something I did alone until after my divorce. Finding partners who were more experienced with squirting, who knew different techniques and more importantly were patient, allowed me to experience squirting with someone else, which is definitely a deeper level of pleasure. I have yet to meet a man who doesn't orgasm quickly and intensely when he feels a woman squirting while he's inside of her.

Some women don't believe they can ejaculate and even some men, who have not experienced it, don't think it's truly possible or normal. But I was a late bloomer in the orgasm territory, waiting until my early 20s to first touch myself through masturbation and reach orgasm. If someone so generally out of touch with her body can learn to ejaculate, anyone can.

A Few Things You Should Know

1. Address your emotional health first. For women orgasm is mostly mental. Issues in your relationship, and especially past sexual or other mental trauma, may greatly affect your ability to experience pleasure. It's still possible, but you need to come to a place mentally where you love yourself, your body and know you ARE worthy of pleasure.

2. Squirting is one of the most intense, pleasurable orgasms you'll ever experience, but it's messy. Some women, myself included, have squirting orgasms which produce enough ejaculate to soak through stacks of towels. Purchase a good thick waterproof mattress cover or you'll ruin your mattress. Be prepared to wash lots of laundry as you won't be able to sleep on the bed after you squirt. You can produce A LOT of fluid and it spreads, often times traveling across the length of the bed. Some women produce only a teaspoon while others produce cups. Make sure your partner is prepared for this mess as well. With female ejaculation there isn't just a teeny wet spot from cum, but instead the whole bed may become soaked.

Squirting: It's Easier Than You Think

3. If you haven't found the g-spot, it's time to find it.
The g-spot is well known as an elusive creature, but it
doesn't have to be. While stimulation on other
erogenous spots can produce a squirting orgasm, the
best way is usually through manipulating a woman's
g-spot. Squirting is not necessarily a g-spot orgasm
(you can have one without stimulating the g-spot),
but it is more likely to happen if the g-spot is
stimulated because pressure on the g-spot can help the
fluid come out. For reference, the g-spot is located
about two inches inside the front vaginal wall. It's
easier to find when aroused, so use clitoral
stimulation first before feeling for it. You'll know
you've reached the g-spot when you feel a spongy,
rough patch of tissue. Some claim it feels similar to
the tip of a nose.

4. Female ejaculation comes out of the urethra not
the vagina. It originates in the g-spot, but is pushed
out of the urethra. It is a watery fluid with a bit of an
oily feeling. It's mostly odorless but may have a
slightly musky or sweet smell and it may taste salty or
sweet. It is fairly consistent in its taste, color, smell
and consistency. The g-spot contains
Skenes/Paraurethral glands which makes the fluid (1).
The fluid contains glucose and the enzyme, prostate
acid phosphatase, which is also a major component of
semen as it is comes from the prostate (2). A woman's

g-spot is similar to a man's prostate (1). Female ejaculation mirrors the benefits of prostate massage for men, and ejaculation also cleanses the urethra which can help to prevent urinary tract infections (3). Female ejaculate IS real. Ejaculate is not urine. It's a normal, healthy sexual release.

What Does it Feel Like?

Female ejaculation is one of the most incredible, pleasurable feelings. Unlike a clitoral orgasm, the pleasure is not centralized, but instead it extends throughout your body. It's an ultimate release, a deep feeling with lots of warmth and wetness. Your whole body experiences contractions, often for minutes, and some people feel like jello afterward, unable to move. Imagine if a man had an orgasm, but never ejaculated. It would feel incomplete. When a woman has an orgasm without ejaculation it feels incomplete, but until she experiences ejaculation she will not understand because it's all she's ever known. A squirting orgasm is unlike anything a woman has ever experienced. It is the most powerful orgasm of her life.

The Importance of a Supportive Partner

Every woman has the ability and the equipment available to squirt. BUT not every woman has a supportive partner or she is willing to overcome her own inhibitions or mental blocks. Some women do not realize they can ejaculate because they are missing their bodies' cues. But every woman can experience female ejaculation, if squirting is desirable to them.

A supportive partner is key. Some partners do not have the patience, nor do they see the value in pleasing their partner. If this is the case, get a new partner! Or have an honest discussion with your current partner. The partners I've had who have pleasured me the most, who have been the most patient and giving sexually, were the ones who had unlocked a secret. They understood if the woman receives pleasure there is great reward for the other partner. Sexual pleasure is always heightened for both when the woman is pleasured.

It's Normal

There is nothing abnormal or unhealthy about female ejaculation. As mentioned previously some women ejaculate several cups of fluid. The amount may be affected by how hydrated a woman is, or how much she pushes while ejaculating. In my experience, the more you experience squirting the easier it becomes to do it again, to have an enhanced experience and to increase the amount of fluid produced.

The Tips

Please note while some of these tips mention a male partner, most of these tips are relevant and useful to same sex partners as well.

Tip #1: Stay hydrated. Fluid=fluid. Drink lots of water. You'll need plenty of fluid in your body to ejaculate, and after ejaculation, you'll want to rehydrate. And don't forget the lubrication. Keep everything wet!

Tip #2: Urinate or don't. The tip here is you can choose to do either. If you urinate before sex, you may feel less worried about the fluid you ejaculate being urine. Some experts say women can urinate and ejaculate at the same time (5), but when a woman becomes aroused with ejaculate other experts disagree, saying (like in men) the bladder is closed off (4), making it very unlikely any pee will sneak through. If a woman is worried about urinating during ejaculation she should urinate before sex so when she starts to feel the urge to urinate she won't worry about peeing. If you have a supportive partner and you are not concerned about urinating, sometimes the additional pressure of a fuller bladder can help with squirting. Honestly, sex is dirty, full of all kinds of gross-ish fluids. Squirting, in most cases, is not urination. While there are conflicting opinions on whether it is all ejaculate or if some urine can become mixed in, in most circumstances, it comes out as clear, colorless, has no odor and I'm told it tastes sweet. Why worry about it if there's a bit of urine mixed in with your ejaculate. More than likely it's all cum.

Tip #3: Relax. The key to any orgasm for any women is relaxation. When you get caught up in your head thinking about what you should be doing (work, school, etc), you affect your pleasure level. Orgasm, especially for a women, is all in the head. If she can't get out of her head, it's a hopeless cause.

Tip #4: Stay in the moment, stay present and become in tune with your body. Yoga and meditation helped me to learn more about being present. Since I've started doing hot yoga and exercising daily I've noticed my orgasms becoming better, more intense and easier to obtain. I would guess to say it's due to having a healthier body and being more in tune with my body. Hot yoga also releases toxins, so if you are not regularly working up a sweat and releasing toxins, it can affect your ability to experience pleasure. Love your body!

Squirting: It's Easier Than You Think

Tip #5: Allow pressure to buildup. Try to accomplish at least 1-2 clitoral orgasms first. This increases the pressure and stimulation and again makes it easier to have an orgasm which produces ejaculate. Don't worry if it feels like you need to pee. Push past the urge to pee. Stimulation of the g-spot results in a sensation where you feel as though you need to pee because your brain associates urethra stimulation as a need to pee. But part of the function of an erect urethral sponge is to close off the urethra to prevent urination during sex. If you ignore the sensation and go with it, your brain does the work of realizing the difference. After multiple squirting sessions, both times when I emptied my bladder and times when I did not, I've never peed. If it feels like you are going to pee, it's because you are getting ready to squirt. Some women back off from that feeling in fear they will pee. Let it go. Don't worry about it.

Tip #6: Don't fight it. Bare down, don't tense up, relax your muscles and push outward when you feel as though you are about to orgasm. Do not clench tight. If you tense up when you are about to cum, you may stop it from happening. Often women are taught not to be messy or not to let their inhibitions go. But a woman who experiences ejaculation achieves a major sexual breakthrough where she feels less inhibited sensually.

Tip #7: Use toys, particularly when masturbating.
When you reach orgasm back off initially if it feels
sensitive. Within such sensitivity you are better able to
access the type of orgasm where you can ejaculate.
Continue to masturbate as soon as you can,
stimulating either the g-spot (preferably, although
this can be harder for some women to access on their
own) or stimulate the clitoris. This may feel a little
uncomfortable the first time or so, but it usually
won't as you get used to it. Keep stimulating either
the clitoris or inside allowing the pressure to build-
up. Don't back off. Let go and allow the orgasm to
keep coming. Experiment with different toys to use
during stimulation. While I have personally not had
good luck with any toy labeled a "g-spot stimulator"
they may work with some women. In general
vibrators provide enough of an enhanced stimulation,
making it easier to build up pressure and come to the
point of ejaculation.

Tip #8: Ask for lots of g-spot stimulation from your
partner. The partner should place 1-2 fingers inside
the vagina and use a "come-hither" motion, moving
the fingers back and forth, as though you're
motioning someone to come over to you. Another
way to describe this technique is by envisioning a
hook. The partner inserts two of his fingers into the
woman's vagina, upwards towards her stomach, as

though he's hooked in towards her belly button. This is particularly effective to stimulate the woman if the partner performs oral sex at the same time. For extra stimulation and pressure your partner can use his free hand to press down on the area between your belly button and your pubic mound. Make sure you achieve a few clitoral orgasms before your partner enters your vagina with his penis. Most women have an easier time orgasming from hands and tongue. But if you achieve several orgasms before he enters, the pressure build-up can make it easier for his penis to reach your g-spot. You can try different sexual positions which may make it easier for your partner's penis to stimulate your g-spot. The positions which work will vary with each couple, but some find insertion from the rear (more commonly called doggy-style) or elevating the woman's hips with pillows are helpful to hitting the g-spot with the penis.

Tip #9: Listen for a wet, squishy noise. The distinctive noise is often a precursor to squirting. It sounds as though fluid is building up. Soon after you hear the sound you'll begin to squirt as long as you're not holding back.

Finally, **Tip #10:** Try what works for you. While all women have the same equipment and the same ability to squirt, we're all different in how our bodies respond to stimulation and what works to achieve an orgasm and female ejaculation. Have fun. Play.

A Few Tips for Partners

I can't stress this concept enough....a genuinely patient, loving, supportive, honest, giving partner goes a long way in helping a woman achieve pleasure. A woman's intuition will tell her if your intentions are anything but genuine and she'll react accordingly.

Tip #1: Help her to relax. One of my partners simply told me, "sex is a journey not a destination." It was such a relief to hear he didn't care if it took awhile. Most of the fun is in the journey anyways. His comment was enough to help me relax, to know I was safe, to know he was right there beside me throughout the journey. He was the first person to experience my squirting abilities after my divorce. If the woman tells you she feels like she needs to pee, or she's worried it's taking too long, continue to reassure her it's ok and to let go (her instincts are telling her to hold back). Encourage her and tell her you can't wait until she cums.

Tip #2: Work towards a slow buildup and incorporate lots of foreplay. I have no doubt had partners who knew about the g-spot, but they stimulated it hard and quick. It's a painful feeling that feels good, BUT it does not reach the height of an orgasm which has been nurtured. Aim for slow and gentle, unless of course the woman requests otherwise. This also gives her time to relax, trust and let go. A partner who is loving, kind and patient, cherishing her, will more likely unleash an amazing flood.

Tip #3: Give it time. Discovering is one of the more fun parts of sex with your partner. Squirting is less likely to happen with a casual partner than one you invest in multiple sexual experiences with. But the fun comes in discovering how you work together. Each partner and how you connect varies widely. Allow yourself to fully embrace the moment, letting go, discovering how your bodies move together. If you have sex with the intent to squirt, it likely won't happen.

In Closing....

These tips are meant to give you guidance so you can start to discover how your body can achieve a squirting orgasm. Keep it by your bedside, and pull it out to use as a quick reference as you explore your body. Female ejaculation is a wonderful sensation every woman deserves to experience!

References

1. Wikipedia, 2014, Skene's Gland
http://en.wikipedia.org/wiki/Skene's_gland#cite_not
e-3
Viewed September 2014
2. Whipple, Beverly and Nasserzadeh, Sara, 2010, *The Orgasm Answer Guide*, The John Hopkins University Press, Maryland
3. Holistic Wisdom, 2014, What is Female Ejaculation?
http://www.holisticwisdom.com/services_female-ejaculation_what-is-it.htm
Viewed September 2014
4. YouTube, 2014, G-Spot Stimulation Explained Step by Step
http://youtu.be/NYvrRxdAAMk
Viewed September 2014
5. Columbia Health, 2000, Go Ask Alice:
Distinguishing Between Orgasm and Urination
http://goaskalice.columbia.edu/am-i-coming-or-going-distinguishing-between-orgasm-and-urination
Viewed September 2014

About the Author

R. Leigh began experiencing female ejaculation in her early 30s, when she'd hardly experienced very many orgasms at all. Her sexual past included rape, molestation, a physically abusive marriage, and few sexual experiences which were enjoyable or included a focus on her pleasure.

Her first experience with female ejaculation lead to a several year journey into understanding her own sexuality, where she embraced pleasure and developed an immense amount of knowledge about the squirting orgasm and how it's accomplished. As she learned more, and became much more comfortable with her body, as well as accepted the fact she deserved pleasure, she also learned more about the role a holistic view plays in sexuality.

Her goal is to share knowledge of female ejaculation with others, particularly woman, to help them understand the strong connection a healthy mind, body and spirit has to pleasurable female sexuality. A healthy sex life is not only crucial to strengthening the connection with your partner, but it's also beneficial to a woman's physical and mental health.

Made in the USA
Columbia, SC
15 July 2018